A Complete Guide to Carp Fishing for Beginners

PAUL DUFFIELD

CONTENTS

INTRODUCTION

The term 'carp fishing' refers to the pursuit of specimen sized carp to the exclusion of other species.

This full colour illustrated guide to carp fishing contains everything the beginner needs to know, from buying the right tackle and choosing the best type of carp water for a beginner, to the tackle, baits and techniques that will make you a successful carp angler.

Fully illustrated chapters explain tackle and bait, with diagrams and instructions for making carp rigs, advice on casting and how to play, land and safely release carp.

Tactics for catching stillwater and river carp are covered, together with tips for stalking, night fishing, long stay sessions and winter carp fishing.

Like any sport carp fishing takes time and practice to learn, but if you pick the right fishery and approach it correctly using the information in this book, there is every possibility that you could catch a carp on your first trip!

If you are a complete beginner and have never fished before, or you are an experienced coarse angler who wants to take up carp fishing, this book will tell you everything you need to know.

ABOUT CARP

While there is more than one species of carp present in Britain and Ireland and several more species around the world, the species of interest to carp anglers is the 'common carp' (Cyprinus carpio).

This species is native to mainland Europe and Asia, but has been domesticated over many centuries and introduced to many countries.

Common carp were bred as a food fish in China as far back as the 5th century BC and for over 1,000 years have also been bred as ornamental fish. The Koi, a popular pond fish in the UK, is one result of this selective breeding.

While the natural form of the common carp is to be fully scaled, variations which had few or no scales were selectively bred for food as they require less preparation prior to cooking.

The common carp is believed to have been first introduced into Britain in the 1300's and since then it has successfully colonised stillwaters and slow moving rivers throughout the country.

Due to selective breeding and subsequent interbreeding of different populations, the common carp can vary widely in appearance. Carp anglers have names for these variations, such as 'fully scaled' to describe carp of natural appearance, 'mirror carp' which have a random pattern of large scales, 'linear carp' which have a single row of scales along the lateral line and 'leather' carp which have few or no scales.

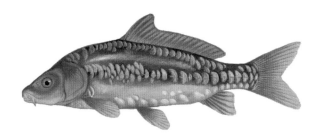

Some anglers differentiate between domesticated common carp that they refer to as 'King carp' and a smaller growing variety known as 'wild carp' or 'wildies'. The latter are slimmer and more streamlined and are considered to be descended without interbreeding from the original strain first introduced to Britain.

Irrespective of appearance, all variations are recognised as a single species and appear only once in the British and Irish record fish lists.

The current British carp record stands at 67lb 14oz (30 .618kg), a fish known as 'Two Tone' which has subsequently died. The Irish record stands at 29lb 13oz (13.522kg)

In recent years, an ornamental strain of the common carp, known as 'ghost carp' has been introduced into many British waters. Ghost carp have the appearance of a common carp, but are silvery white in colour.

Other species of carp present in Britain are the grass carp (Ctenopharyngodon idella) which can grow to over 40lb (18kg) crucian carp (Carassius carassius), a much smaller growing species that rarely exceeds 4lb (1.8 kg) and the F1, a hybrid between the common carp and crucian carp that typically grows to less than 10lb (4.535kg). The F1 is a popular fish with match anglers and has been introduced into many commercial carp fisheries.

WHERE TO FISH FOR CARP

Carp anglers have a wide range of waters to choose from these days and you should be able to find several waters to fish for carp in your local area.

These range from hard waters containing small numbers of large carp, through mixed fisheries and club lakes with carp among the stock of coarse fish to commercial carp fisheries containing large numbers of carp with some weighing up to low double figures.

Some waters are controlled by syndicates and have waiting lists, but for the beginner to carp fishing, a day ticket or club water would be a better choice to learn the basics of carp fishing, leaving the harder, more specialist waters until you have a season or two of carp fishing under your belt.

While commercial carp fisheries and club lakes are stocked and maintained with the general coarse angler and match angler in mind, most contain larger carp that have grown on from the original stock fish.

Most anglers on these waters will use general coarse fishing or match fishing techniques such as float fishing to target the carp of a few pounds that make up the majority of the stock, but carp fishing methods can be used to target the larger specimens.

You will catch smaller carp too, but while you are becoming familiar with your tackle and honing your skills, hooking and landing carp from a few pounds to low double figures will all add to your experience and stand you in good stead when you hook your first specimen sized carp.

For your first season, or at least the first few months of it, I suggest that you concentrate on building up your skills and experience on waters where you can reasonably expect to catch several carp in a day session, with the realistic possibility that on occasions you will catch a fish of 10 pounds (4.5kg) or more.

You may not find the prospect of only catching fish up to low double figures very exciting if you have read about the much larger fish that are featured in the angling press every week, but when you catch your first double figure carp I think you will find it quite enough to handle!

Your local tackle shop should be able to recommend local waters suitable for a beginner to carp fishing and advise on the tactics, rigs and baits that are successful on those waters.

CARP FISHING TACKLE

It can be very expensive to put together even a mid-priced carp fishing outfit, especially if you intend to fish through the night or for sessions of two days or more. I have seen articles in the angling press suggesting that a beginner needs to spend £1,000 or more just for the basics.

If your budget will stretch to that the by all means buy the best equipment that you can afford, but it is quite possible to put together a carp fishing outfit that will be perfectly adequate for your first season or two for substantially less.

You will inevitably, as every angler does, add to your tackle over time and as you become more experienced and move on to new waters to target larger fish, you can upgrade your rods, reels and other equipment as required.

CHOOSING A ROD FOR CARP FISHING

Most carp anglers fish with two or more rods so that they can fish both a distant swim and one closer to the bank, or fish different baits on each rod.

If you start your carp fishing on well stocked waters as I have suggested, it will not be a problem if you can only afford one rod to begin with. You should be able to find carp and get bites with a single rod set up on such waters without too much difficulty.

There are generally three factors used to describe a carp rod; test curve action and length.

The test curve is an indication of the strength of the rod and is a value from 2.5lb up to 4lb. This is the amount of weight needed to bend the rod to 90 degrees if the weight is suspended from the tip and the rod is held horizontally.

The action, usually described as through action, medium action or fast action, is determined by the taper of the rod and describes how the rod will bend when under stress.

A through action rod will bend evenly to throughout its whole length, a fast action rod mainly at the tip and a medium action rod is between the two.

Carp rods are generally available in lengths from 11ft to 13ft although some manufacturers do supply longer or shorter rods.

A medium action rod of 12ft in length with a test curve of 2.5lb or 2.75lb costing around £50 is a good all round rod for a beginner and will be suitable for the types of waters I have suggested you target initially.

CHOOSING A REEL FOR CARP FISHING

You will need a fixed spool reel with free spool capability which is a special mode operated using a switch or a lever that allows line to be pulled off the reel while the bail arm is closed.

Without free spool capability there would be the risk of the rod being pulled into the water if a large fish picked up the bait and swam away strongly (this is known as a run).

As soon as the handle is turned, the free spool mode is disengaged and the reel functions like any normal fixed spool reel, further line being given by winding the handle backwards or using a slipping clutch.

Reels with free spool capability were originally supplied by the company Shimano under the Baitrunner brand name, but free spool reels are now available from many reel manufacturers.

Budget priced free spools are available from around £10, but a reel in the £20 to £25 price range will be better and last longer.

PARTS OF A FREE SPOOL REEL

1: Pick up or bail
2: Reel foot
3: Support arm
4: Free spool lever
5: Tension adjustment
6: Handle
7: Anti-reverse switch
8: Spool
9: Clutch adjustment

LINE FOR YOUR REEL

For the types of waters I have suggested you fish, a nylon monofilament line of 12lb (5.5kg) breaking strain will be suitable. Make sure you buy enough line in a single continuous run to fill the spool to avoid unnecessary knots which could impede casting.

LOADING LINE ON TO THE REEL

Line should be loaded on to the reel so that it almost reaches the edge of the spool.

A reel that is not loaded with enough line will be difficult to cast with while an overfilled spool will result in tangles.

UNDERFILLED   OVERFILLED   CORRECT

If your reel has a deep spool and your main line is not enough to fill it, you will need to put some backing line on first.

LANDING NET

Many clubs and fisheries will insist that you  are properly equipped if you are targeting carp and will specify a minimum net size. This is likely to be at least 36 inches (90 cm) which is quite large enough for carp you will catch on most club waters and commercial fisheries.

The difference in price between a 36 inch net and a larger one of 42 inches (106 cm) is not great so if you are intending to fish waters with larger fish later on you may prefer to buy the larger size.

Carp nets usually comprise 3 parts; the net itself, a spreader block and a handle. Make sure that you get a strong spreader block that fits the arms of the net. Spreader blocks are available made of plastic or metal. Personally I prefer the metal ones as I have found them to be more robust.

The handle should be strong and at least 6 feet (182 cm) long. Avoid the lightweight telescopic handles made for coarse and match fishing as they are not strong enough.

UNHOOKING MAT

Carp should always be supported on a large, thick padded mat for unhooking. A wide range  of good quality mats is available and you should have no difficulty in obtaining one for a few pounds.

Lay the mat out ready before you start fishing rather than waiting until you have caught a carp.

FORCEPS

Forceps are inexpensive and much better for removing hooks from carp than fingers. They are easily mislaid during a session so I suggest you buy a few pairs so you can keep one in a pocket, one with your terminal tackle and one with your unhooking mat.

CARP CARE KITS

Many fisheries require you to have antiseptic to treat the carp after unhooking. There are a number of good quality carp care kits available from several manufacturers.

WEIGH SLINGS AND SCALES

A weigh sling of soft material should always be used to weigh carp. One that zips up to retain the carp while weighing is safest and easiest for the beginner to use.

Good quality scales will be needed to weigh carp accurately such as those made by Reuben Heaton, Avon or Chub.

ROD RESTS AND ROD PODS

Rod rests and rod pods are used to suspend rods above the bank at the correct angle to the water for the free spool system to operate correctly.

Whether you choose to buy rod rests or pods will depend on the banks of the waters you intend to fish.

Rod rests have a spike or point that is pushed into the bank and a threaded connector at the other end to take rod rest heads and alarms.

Two rod rests are required for each rod, with either a rod rest head and an alarm or two rod rest heads for each pair.

Rod pods are of free standing frame construction which can make them difficult to set up and use on uneven banks, but they work better on hard ground where pushing in a bank stick would be difficult.

BITE INDICATOR BOBBINS

Bobbins are clipped on to the line a little before the alarm or front rod rest. They provide a visual indication as a bite develops and if you are using an alarm, they provide weight to keep the line on the roller wheel.

It is best to get bobbins that have a facility for adding extra weight so you can adjust the tension on the line to suit different fishing conditions.

BITE ALARMS

Bite alarms were originally invented for night fishing because visual bite indicators could not be seen in the dark, but nowadays many carp anglers use them during the day too.

If you only intend to fish in daylight, you can manage without buying alarms and instead watch the bobbins constantly for signs of a bite.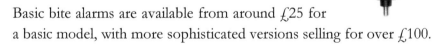

Basic bite alarms are available from around £25 for a basic model, with more sophisticated versions selling for over £100.

LUGGAGE

You will need luggage to carry your fishing tackle plus other items such as bait, food, drink and clothing to your swim.

If you intend to carry your rods already made up with reels and rigs, which many carp anglers do, a quiver will be fine for carrying your rods plus other items such as rod rests, rod pods, landing nets, umbrellas and shelters.

A quiver can still be used for carrying rods that are not made up, but you may prefer to use a rod holdall instead.

Quivers and rod holdalls are available in many sizes and prices so you should have no trouble finding one to suit your budget.

All other items are most conveniently carried in a shoulder bag or rucksack. It is surprising how the bulk and weight of everything you need to carry to your swim can mount up, so make sure you get one that is large enough to take everything comfortably and that it has well padded straps for comfort. Again, these are available across a wide range of sizes and prices.

CHAIRS AND BEDCHAIRS

You will be spending a lot of time sitting down while carp fishing, so a comfortable chair is essential.

Unless you will only be fishing on level banks, you will need a chair with adjustable legs. A padded back and seat area will also help you to be comfortable for long periods.

Some rucksacks are designed to have a chair clipped on to them so you do not have to carry the chair separately, but if you are using a shoulder bag or a rucksack that does not have this facility, a chair with a carrying strap will be more convenient.

When choosing a chair remember that you are going to have to carry it to your swim, so weight is important.

SHELTERS

If you are only planning to fish daylight sessions of a few hours, an umbrella or basic carp shelter will be sufficient to provide protection from the rain.

If you are intending to fish longer sessions of two days or more, you will need a 'bivvy' to provide more substantial protection from the elements, especially during the colder months.

BAIT TABLE

While not essential, a small bait table is convenient for keeping baits, tools, spare rig components and drinks next to your fishing chair.

They are light and compact to carry. Choose one with adjustable legs so it will be level on sloping and uneven banks.

TACKLE AND RIG SYSTEM BOX

You will need to carry quite a lot of tools and small items for making rigs and you will find it much more convenient to keep these items in a tackle and rig system box.

These are plastic boxes with moveable compartments that house smaller compartment boxes inside them, allowing you to organise all of your tools and tackle neatly and conveniently.

Tackle and rig system boxes are available from many manufacturers in a wide range of sizes and are priced from just a few pounds.

TOOLS AND TERMINAL TACKLE

There are many tools and accessories for carp fishing, some of which are essential and some of which can be useful or save time when making rigs or baiting hooks.

Terminal tackle is the collective term for anything that goes on the line to make up a fishing rig, including hooks, weights, swivels, connectors and many other items.

Over the last few years there have been significant developments and advancements in carp fishing rigs and the components that are used to construct them.

Many tackle manufacturers have their own systems and it is not practical to list every item of rig building equipment available. In this section I will list essential and useful items including all of the components required to make any of the rigs listed in this book.

As you become more experienced you will develop your own preferences for tools and components and can add to these items as required.

LINE CUTTER

A line cutter or sharp nail scissors are useful for neatly trimming knots.

BRAID SCISSORS

Braid is too strong to be cut with ordinary scissors or line cutters so if you intend to use braid you need a pair of braid scissors.

RIG PULLER

A rig puller is a useful accessory for testing that knots and rigs are sound and tight so you can fish with confidence that your rig wont let you down when a carp takes the bait.

LOOP TYER

A loop tyer helps you to consistently tie neat loops of a uniform size.

KNOT PICKER

A knot picker is a useful accessory for un-picking and tidying knots in rigs.

HOOK SHARPENER

Hooks can be blunted against stones and other obstructions. With a hook sharpener you can re-touch the point and avoid having to change the hook.

BAIT DRILL

A bait drill is used to drill a hole through hard baits so they can be attached to a hair rig.

BAITING NEEDLE

A baiting needle is used to attach drilled and soft baits to hair rigs.

STRINGER NEEDLE

A stringer needle is a longer version of a baiting needle designed to thread several baits such as boilies on to soluble PVA string. The string of boilies is attached to the rig and cast out, leaving your hook bait next to some free offerings after the PVA string has dissolved.

BAIT STOPS

Bait stops are used to trap drilled baits against the loop of a hair rig.

BOILIE SPIKES

As an alternative to threading the hair rig through a boilie and trapping it against the loop with a bait stop you can include a boilie spike inside the loop of the hair.

These are available in plastic or metal and simply push into the boilie to hold it in place.

BAIT BANDS

These are silicon bands available in a range of sizes that can be used to attach hard baits such pellets, or large baits such as bread flake to the hook.

PELLET BANDER

A pellet bander is used to temporarily stretch a silicon bait band to make it easier to slip over hard pellets.

BAIT PUNCH

A bait punch is used to cut uniform sized hook baits from luncheon meat.

PVA TAPE AND PVA STRING

PVA tape and string is a soluble material that can be used to attach free offerings of your hook bait to your rig using a stringer needle and can also be used to tie PVA bags.

PVA BAGS

PVA bags are used when you want to get a more substantial amount of bait in close proximity to your hook bait than is possible with a PVA stringer.

Solid PVA bags can be used for a mix of small offerings and can also include liquid flavours. Mesh PVA bags can also be used for dry baits and have the advantage that they will dissolve more quickly than solid bags.

CATAPULT

A catapult is useful for firing out free offerings of your hook bait if you are fishing further out than you can throw accurately.

HOOKS

Hooks sizes are given as a number, the higher the number, the larger the hook..

At one time hooks were of a similar size irrespective of pattern but that is no longer the case and hooks with the same numeric size value can vary significantly in actual size between patterns and manufacturers.

The difference is not usually as much as the next hook size up or down though, so treat the size given a general guide.

You can buy hooks already tied to line in many configurations. Hook links tied with nylon, fluorocarbon and braid, incorporating hair rig loops, bait bands, bait spikes and other specialist components are all available.

If you buy quality rigs from a leading manufacturer they will perform exactly as intended. As well as helping to smooth out the learning curve by giving you less to learn initially, you can also examine these hook links to better understand how they are constructed when you are ready to tie your own.

The only disadvantage with buying pre-tied hook links is that unless your carry a very large selection, you will not have the flexibility that being able to tie your own will give you. For this reason its a good idea to have a good selection of loose hooks and hook link components so that you can make up your own if you don't have a suitable ready tied rig available.

As you will initially be targeting carp from several pounds up to double figures in weight, you do not need to carry the range of hooks that generalist coarse anglers do. A selection of hooks in sizes 6, 8 and 10 plus 12 if you intend to fish small baits such as a single grain of sweetcorn should cover your needs.

For hair rigs, the size 6 hook is suitable for boilies and pellets of 20mm or more, the size 8 for boilies and pellets of 16mm to 20mm or 2 to 3 grains of sweetcorn and the size 10 for smaller boilies and pellets or 2 grains of sweetcorn.

When putting the bait directly on the hook, the size 6 is suitable for large pieces of bread crust or paste or a whole lobworm, the size 8 for smaller pieces of bread crust or paste or a dendrobaena worm and the size 10 for two or three grains of sweetcorn or up to 3 soft pellets depending on size.

For other baits, use the above as a guide to the size of hook you should use based on the size of the bait.

Hooks are available both with and without barbs. It is rare these days to find stillwater fisheries that allow the use of barbed hooks and they are not really necessary, so you should make sure that all of the hooks you buy are barbless.

Over time you will develop your own preferences for hook patterns, but to begin with you do not need to carry a large range of hook patterns for tying your own rigs.

A selection in the sizes given above in a single pattern will be fine and you can experiment with hooks in other patterns and from other manufacturers as you become more experienced.

A strong carp hook with an inward pointing eye similar to the one pictured is a good general pattern to choose.

LINE FOR HOOK LINKS

For the types of waters I have suggested you fish initially there is no need for you to make up hook links with specialist lines or braid.

A spool of good quality 10lb nylon monofilament will be suitable and you will find it much easier to tie hook links with nylon than with fluorocarbon or braid.

SWIVELS

Swivels help to avoid line twist and are an essential component of many rigs.

RUBBER BEADS

Rubber beads are used as a shock absorber are an essential component of many rigs.

FLOAT STOPS

Although designed to be used in place of stop knots for sliding float rigs, float stops are a quick, convenient and safe way to semi-fix the position of components on rigs.

You will see examples of their use in the carp rigs chapter.

SAFETY LEGER CLIPS AND TAIL SLEEVES

These are plastic clips that are used in conjunction with a swivel to attach leger weights to rigs.

They are designed to allow the weight to be ejected from the rig if it becomes snagged while playing a fish and to prevent it from remaining attached to a fish in the event of a line break.

Tail sleeves push over the end of the clips to provide a neat and streamlined rig.

SILICON TUBING

Silicon tubing can be used to hold hair rigs in place along the shank of a hook and to cover components such as swivels to stop tangles.

STIFF RIG TUBING

Sometimes called anti-tangle tubing, this is sometimes using to stiffen or bend parts of a rig to avoid the hook link tangling on the main line during casting.

SHRINK TUBING

Heat shrink tubing is sometimes used to alter the angle of the hook on the line, for example to improve hooking efficiency by putting a curve in the hook link.

LEAD CORE LEADERS

Lead core leaders are sometimes used between the main line and terminal tackle, to anchor the line to the bottom where it is out of the way of any carp in the swim.

You can buy lead core leaders ready made with a loop either end or make your own.

Some fisheries do not allow the use of lead core so check the rules before you use it.

LEGER WEIGHTS

Often referred to as lead weights, these are used to provide casting weight and to anchor the rig in position on the bottom. When fishing rivers, the weight holds the rig in place against the current. When using semi-fixed bolt rigs on stillwaters the weight causes resistance when a carp takes the bait, hopefully inducing a run.

Leger weights are available in a wide range of shapes and sizes, usually starting at around 1 ounce. Depending on the style, they are either attached to the line using a ring or swivel located at the top, or by threading the line through a hole running through the weight.

The heaviest weight you can use is dictated by the test curve of your rod, the general rule being that you can cast 1 ounce of lead per pound of test curve, i.e. a rod with a test curve of 2.5lb could cast a maximum weight of 2.5oz.

Many rods now have the maximum safe casting weight printed on them and it is possible to cast heavier weights than the general rule would suggest if this is done with care and with a more gentle cast than you would use if you were aiming for maximum distance.

You should carry a selection of designs and sizes to cope with a range of fishing situations but keep in mind that it doesn't take many weights to add a couple of pounds of carrying weight to your tackle.

If you have to walk any distance, consider leaving any weights you don't expect to use at home or in the car.

Weights and the names they are sold under can vary between manufacturers, but the following are the main types you will need:

PEAR

The pear weight is reasonably streamlined so can be cast quite long distances and its compact shape provides better resistance to a biting carp when using a semi-fixed bolt rig.

It is a good general purpose leger weight and will work well in most conditions.

FLAT PEAR

The flat pear weight holds well on sloping or hard bottoms and is a good choice for fishing semi-fixed bolt rigs at short and medium range.

SQUARE PEAR

The square pear weight is designed to provide better casting distance than the flat pear, while retaining much of its ability to hold on well on the bottom.

DISTANCE BOMB

This is a much more streamlined weight than the pear, designed to give the maximum possible casting distance.

While this weight will not grip the bottom as well as the pear, it will allow you to reach fish that would otherwise be out of range.

GRIPPER

The gripper weight provides maximum grip for minimum weight making it ideal for use on rivers where long casting is not required, but a strong grip is needed to combat fast currents.

SHOT

Shot is used to weight floats and is also useful for fine tuning rigs, for example by adding one or two shot to a free-line rig to add casting weight or anchor the hook link to the bottom.

The sizes you are most likely to use are SG, SSG, AAA and BBB, but a dispenser containing most of these plus some smaller sizes is inexpensive and worth carrying so you have the smaller sizes if you need them .

Shot was originally made from lead and many anglers still refer to it as lead shot, but the use of lead in all but the smallest sizes of shot was made illegal in the U.K. in 1986, since which time non-toxic alternatives have to be used.

There is a wide range of non-toxic shot available, but make sure that you get a good quality brand of soft shot which can usually be identified by a light grey colour. This is less likely to damage line and is easier to remove for re-use.

TUNGSTEN PUTTY

Tungsten putty is a heavy pliable material than can be moulded on to the line or on to swivels to balance a rig or to pin a hook link to the bottom.

It is available in different colours so you can match it to the bed of the water you are fishing.

SWIMFEEDERS

Swimfeeders do not play a large part in carp
fishing.

The exception is the method feeder which is
designed to allow a hook bait to be fished among a mix of ground
bait and loose feed.

FISHING FLOATS

Although you will probably use legering techniques and rigs for most
of your carp fishing, there may be occasions when you want to use a
float rig so its a good idea to have some in your tackle box.

The following floats are the types that are most useful for carp
fishing.

CARP CONTROLLER

The carp controller is used for fishing floating baits on the surface of
stillwater fisheries.

STRAIGHT WAGGLER

A straight waggler float is good for stalking and fishing the margins
using the lift method.

PELLET WAGGLER

A thicker and shorter version of the straight waggler.

LOADED PELLET WAGGLER

A self-cocking version of the pellet waggler.

PELLET WAGGLER ADAPTERS

Pellet waggler adapters are used to attach loaded pellet wagglers to the line.

PLUMMETS

These are small weights incorporating either a strip of cork or a hinge to hold the hook while lowering the tackle into the swim so you can set the float at the correct depth.

You will not need these for most of your carp fishing but they are useful when setting up a lift method float rig for fishing in the margins.

ADDITIONAL ITEMS

A penknife and a small pair of pliers are handy accessories to keep tucked away somewhere in your kit. You won't use them every trip, but they can be very useful when you need to do running repairs to reels, bank sticks and other tackle.

NIGHT FISHING EXTRAS AND ESSENTIALS

For night fishing and longer sessions you need a few additional items.

TORCH

A torch is essential to find things in the dark. LED torches will provide enough illumination in your immediate area well without lighting up the whole lake and have much better battery life than conventional torches.

Make sure you have a spare set of batteries in case you need to change them.

HEAD TORCH

An LED torch attached to a flexible band that you can wear on your head leaves both hands free for tying rigs and unhooking carp in the dark.

Again, make sure you have spare batteries with you.

SLEEPING BAG

It can get very cold at night, even during the summer so you need a sleeping bag to keep you warm at night.

A lightweight sleeping bag should be all you need in the warmer months, but if you plan to fish at night in autumn or winter, a thicker sleeping bag and possibly an additional cover will be needed.

COOKING EQUIPMENT

While a flask of tea or coffee and some sandwiches is enough to keep you going for a few hours during the day, a freshly made hot drink and a hot meal will help to keep you warm and motivated on cold night sessions.

A small compact stove, kettle and cooking pan take up little room in your luggage, but make sure you have enough fuel to last the session.

LARGE WATER BOTTLE

You will need a large enough water bottle to carry water for making hot drinks.

COOL BAG

A cool bag will keep food, milk and bait fresh for long periods.

SPARE CLOTHING

Take extra clothing such as a fleece or jumper for when it starts to get colder in the evening.

BEDCHAIR POUCH

Many companies offer a compact pouch that can be attached to chairs and bedchairs.

These are useful for keeping items such as your phone, keys and wallet as well as fishing tools such as baiting needles secure and close to hand.

CARP RIGS

This chapter contains diagrams and instructions for several popular carp fishing rigs.

Some of these rigs, such as the method feeder rig and pellet waggler rig are more suited to heavily stocked commercial carp fisheries, but they can be effective techniques for the specialist carp angler in the right conditions.

There is a huge array of specialised components for carp rig construction with many manufacturers having their own systems. To keep things simple, the rigs in this chapter are constructed using generic components but will work just as well if constructed with components of equivalent functionality.

When constructing rigs, make sure that they will not be a danger to carp in the event of the line breaking. In particular ensure that wherever a break occurs the leger or swimfeeder will not remain attached to the hook link.

RUNNING LEGER RIG

This is a very simple rig to tie and has accounted for many carp catches.

To construct the rig, slide a leger weight on to the main line followed by a rig bead and tie a swivel to the end of the main line. Complete the rig by tying a hair rig hook link to the swivel.

This rig presents very little resistance to biting carp and is ideal on waters that are not heavily fished.

SEMI-FIXED BOLT RIG

This rig is a safe version of the bolt rig, designed to provide resistance as soon as a fish takes the bait causing it to either run, providing positive indication of a bite, or hook itself against the weight of the leger.

To construct the rig, thread the main line through a tail sleeve and safety clip and attach a swivel to the end of the main line. Push the swivel into the safety clip, attach a weight and push the sleeve over the end of the clip.

Complete the rig by tying a hair link hook length to the swivel.

If the leger becomes snagged when playing a fish it will break free from the safety clip. In the event of a break off, either the swivel will pull free from the safety clip or the leger will pull free to ensure that the fish is not tethered to the leger.

If you prefer not to use a safety clip, a similar rig can be constructed by threading the weight directly on to the mainline, with a float stop and rig bead either side.

HELICOPTER RIG

The helicopter rig is one of the earliest specialist carp rigs and was designed for long range tangle free casting. It is so named because the hook link revolves around the main line during the cast.

There are many variants of the helicopter rig and many companies have developed components specifically for its construction, but a simple version of this rig can be easily constructed using basic components.

To construct a simple version of this rig, thread a float stop on to the line, followed by a bead, a swivel, another bead and another float stop.

A leger is tied to the end of the main line and a hair rig hook link to the swivel. Push the float stops, beads and swivel down to the leger to lock everything in place but make sure that the swivel can move freely around the main line.

Some anglers prefer to construct this to rig using tubing pushed through the beads, dispensing with the float stops, or with specialised rig components.

CHOD RIG

The chod rig is a variant of the helicopter rig designed to be fished with a buoyant bait over bottoms of soft silt or leaf and weed debris.

To construct a simple version of the chod rig, thread a float stop on to the line, followed by a bead, a swivel, another bead and another float stop. A leger is tied to the end of the main line and a short stiff hair rig hook link is tied to the swivel.

Push the float stops, beads and swivel together to lock everything in place far enough up the line to ensure that the bait is not pulled below the silt and surface debris.

ZIG RIG

The zig rig is designed to fish a buoyant bait above the bottom of the water and can be fished at any depth all the way up to the surface.

There are many ways to tie a zig rig, but to ensure maximum flexibility with this method you need to be able to vary the distance above the bottom that the bait is suspended so you can react to changes in the depth the carp are feeding at during a session.

A simple version of the zig rig based on the running leger rig can be constructed by the addition of float stops to regulate the fishing depth.

To construct the rig, slide a float stop, bead and leger weight on to the main line followed by another rig bead and float stop. Tie a swivel to the end of the main line and complete the rig by tying a hair rig hook link to the swivel.

Use a buoyant bait with this rig such as a large popup boilie.

The depth at which the bait is fished can be adjusted by sliding the float stops, bead and hook link swivel up or down the line.

MARGIN FREE-LINING RIG

When stalking in the margins a simple free-lining rig which is basically nothing more than a hair rig hook link can be effective.

To construct the rig attach a swivel to the main line and tie on a hair rig hook link of up to 6 inches (15 cm) in length.

This rig can be effective with no weight on the line, but if you want to pin down the hook link to the bottom, small shots or blobs of tungsten putty can be attached between the swivel and the hook.

METHOD FEEDER RIG

The method feeder rig is designed to allow a hook bait to be fished among a mix of ground bait and loose feed.

To construct the rig, thread one or two floats stops on to the line, followed by the feeder and tie a swivel to the end of the main line. Tie very short hook link of about 3 inches (8 cm) to the other end of the swivel and push the float stop up to the feeder to lock everything in place.

A hard core of groundbait is moulded on to the feeder frame and the baited hook is pushed into the edge of this layer. A softer layer of groundbait containing samples of the hook bait is then moulded around the feeder.

When the feeder reaches the bottom, the groundbait will begin to break up, much like a ball of ground bait. On heavily stocked waters carp will attack the ball and eat anything that is dislodged, including your hook bait.

Many special 'method mix' ground baits have been developed for this method and you should find a good selection available at your local tackle shop.

CARP CONTROLLER FLOAT RIG

The carp controller float rig is suitable for fishing a floating bait when fish are feeding on the surface.

The rig is simple to construct; the main line is threaded through the eye at the top of the float, followed by one or two rubber beads that act as a shock absorber.

A size 8 swivel is then tied to the end of the main line and the hook link is tied to the other side of the swivel.

Hair rigged floating baits such as floating pellets and bread work well with this method. Small amounts of feed should be introduced regularly. If you feed too much, wind may carry the excess bait out of your swim, followed by the fish.

Bites are detected either by watching the float for movement or watching the end of the rod tip. Bites are usually aggressive and result in the fish being hooked without the need to strike.

LIFT METHOD FLOAT RIG

The lift method float rig is an effective rig for stalking and margin fishing.

As the fish may not move far after picking up the hook bait, a bite may not be seen easily using a standard waggler rig.

The float is locked on to the line using two small shots or a length of silicon tubing.

A single shot, large enough to set the float, is placed 2 to 6 inches (5 to 15 cm) from the hook.

The depth must be accurately plumbed so that when the large shot is sitting on the bottom of the water, only the top of the float is visible.

When a carp takes the bait, the shot will be lifted off the bottom and the float will come up in the water signalling the bite.

PELLET WAGGLER FLOAT RIG

The pellet waggler was developed for fishing near the surface on commercial carp fisheries.

They are normally used with hair rigs to fish with banded or drilled pellets as the bait.

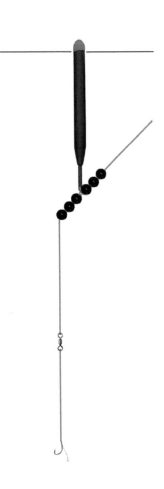

The hook length is attached to the main line using a small swivel to avoid line twist.

All of the shot required to set the float is used to lock it on the line by placing equal numbers of shot either side of the float.

As large shots are required, some anglers place thin silicon tubing either side of the float and attach the shot to the tubing to avoid the shot damaging the line.

A depth of around 2 feet (60 cm) is a good starting point, but be prepared to adjust this until you find the depth at which the fish are feeding.

LOADED PELLET WAGGLER FLOAT RIG

The loaded pellet waggler is a variation on the standard pellet waggler that does not require any shot on the line.

Instead, a specialised pellet float adapter is used to lock the float in place.

In all other respects, the rig is the same as the standard pellet waggler rig.

The hook length is attached to the main line using a small swivel to avoid line twist.

A depth of around 2 feet (60 cm) is a good starting point, but be prepared to adjust this until you find the depth at which the fish are feeding.

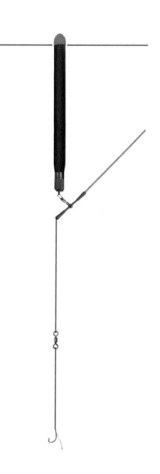

...

KNOTS FOR CARP FISHING

There are many knots that are suitable for fishing, but you need only learn a few to begin with to be equipped for any fishing situation.

When tying knots it is a good idea to moisten the knot before pulling tight as this will lubricate the line and prevent it from being weakened by heat damage caused by friction.

KNOTS FOR MAKING LOOPS

The two knots below are easy to tie and are suitable for making loops in line.

SURGEON'S LOOP KNOT

Double over the line to form a loop. Form a second loop and pass the doubled end of the line through the second loop three times. Moisten, pull tight and trim.

STEP 1   STEP 2   STEP 3

BLOOD LOOP KNOT

Double over the line to form a loop. Twist the loop and pass the doubled end of the line back through the first loop as shown in step 2 below. Moisten, pull tight and trim.

STEP 1   STEP 2   STEP 3

KNOTS FOR JOINING LINE

The knots in this chapter are used for joining line such as the main line to a hook link.

LOOP METHOD

The simplest method of joining two lengths of line is to use two loops tied using either the surgeon's loop knot or a blood loop knot.

Thread the loops together as shown in step 1 below and pull tight.

STEP 1   STEP 2

BLOOD KNOT

The blood knot is used to joint lines of similar diameter.

Wrap one length of line around another to form interlocked loops. Twist both loops and pass the standing ends back through the loops where they connect. Pass the standing ends through each of the loops. Moisten, pull tight and trim.

STEP 1   STEP 2   STEP 3

ALBRIGHT KNOT

The albright knot is used to join lines that are not of similar diameter.

Form a loop in the thicker of the two lines. Pass the end of the thinner line through the loop and wrap it neatly around itself and the loop ten times. Pass the end back through the loop so it exits on the same side it entered. Moisten, pull tight and trim.

STEP 1   STEP 2   STEP 3   STEP 4

KNOTS FOR ATTACHING HOOKS AND SWIVELS

Hooks and swivels can be attached to the line using the knots illustrated below.

SNELL KNOT

This knot can be used to tie either eyed or spade end hooks. If you are tying an eyed hook, first pass the line through the eye of the hook.

Hold the line parallel to the hook shank, form a loop and pass the standing end of the line through the loop five or six times. Moisten, pull tight and trim.

| STEP 1 | STEP 2 | STEP 3 |

TUCKED HALF BLOOD KNOT

The tucked half blood knot can be used to attach eyed hooks and swivels to line.

Pass the line through the eye of the hook or swivel and twist the line as shown in step 1. Twist the loop and pass the standing end of the line back through the loop next to the eye. Pass the standing end of the line through the loop just created. Moisten, pull tight and trim.

| STEP 1 | STEP 2 | STEP 3 |

THE KNOTLESS KNOT FOR TYING HAIR RIGS

You can buy hair rigs already tied, but it is very easy to make your own using the knotless knot.

The basic hair rig incorporates a loop that is pulled through a bait, such as a boilie, using a baiting needle and locked in place using a bait stop.

To build on the basic form, you can incorporate additional components into the loop such as maggot clips, boilie spikes and bait bands.

TYING THE KNOTLESS KNOT

Tie a loop for the hair. If you want to include a bait band or boilie spike tie it inside the loop.

Pass the free end of the line through the eye of the hook and pull the line through until you have the length of hair you want, taking into account that if you are using a bait band or boilie spike, the bait will sit off the end of the hair whereas a bait secured with a bait stop have part of the hair inside it.

Wrap the free end of the line back down the hook 8 to 10 times.

Finally, take the free end of the line back to the eye of the hook, pass it back through the eye and pull tight.

STEP 1   STEP 2   STEP 3

STOP KNOT

Hold the stop knot material to be used for the stop knot (e.g. line or powergum) parallel to the main line. Fold the stop knot material to form a loop and wrap five turns around both the stop knot material and main line inside the loop you have created. Moisten and pull tight.

STEP 1   STEP 2   STEP 3

ARBOR KNOT

The arbor knot is used to attach line or backing to a reel.

Pass the line or backing around the spool and tie an overhand knot around the free end of the line. Tie a second overhand knot in the free end of the line to act as a stop. Slide the knots down to the spool and pull tight.

STEP 1   STEP 2   STEP 3

CARP BAITS

Many baits can be used to catch carp. A huge range of manufactured baits are available from tackle shops, but there are many other baits you can try too.

BOILIES

The best known bait for modern carp fishing is the boilie. These were originally developed   as hard skinned versions of paste baits to stop the bait being nibbled away by small fish.

Boilies are available in several sizes and a huge range of flavours. They require no preparation, are easy to use and have probably accounted for more large carp captures than any other bait.

Shelf life boilies are readily available in most tackle shops and will keep for months if unopened. They will keep for quite a long time after you have opened them too, so long as they are kept cool and dry, so any not used in a session can be taken home for use next time.

Frozen boilies are also available at some tackle shops and these can be very economical if you buy in bulk and only defrost enough for a session.

There are no hard and fast rules about which colours and flavours work best, any could be successful on a given day, but in winter when carp are less active and less inclined to feed, bright colours and fruity or spicy flavours are preferred by many carp anglers.

Boilies are available in a range of sizes from 10mm to around 25mm and all sizes will catch carp from a few pounds in weight, but for waters suitable for beginners where the carp only grow to low double figures, boilies from 10 to 18mm will be suitable.

As well as sinking boilies which can be used both for feeding and on the hook, it often pays to have some buoyant versions that can be fished popped up above the bed of the lake.

Boilies are too large and hard to be put directly on he hook, so they are fished on a hair rig.

PELLETS

A wide range of pellets are available in tackle shops and the range of flavours available rivals that of boilies.

As with boilies, no one colour or flavour is guaranteed to work best, but as a general rule, avoid pellets with a high oil content such as marine halibut pellets during the colder months.

Pellets can be soft or hard. Soft pellets can be fished on a hair rig or directly on the hook. Hard pellets are hair rigged, either by drilling the pellet and threading it on to the hair, or by attaching it to the hair with a silicon bait band.

PASTE

Paste can be used on its own moulded on to a hook, or wrapped around a boilie to increase the flavour and scent leakage.

Boiles wrapped in paste can also work well on hard fished waters as they have a more ragged appearance than a fresh boilie which may fool a wary carp as it will think that the boilie has been in the water for several days.

Shelf life pastes are available in re-sealable tubs in a wide range of colours and flavours, many of which match the flavours of boilies by the same manufacturer.

PARTICLES

The term particle is used to cover a wide range of small baits such as seeds, nuts, beans and pulses.

Sweetcorn is a favourite particle bait and can be used straight from the tin in its natural yellow form. Flavoured and coloured sweetcorn prepared for fishing is available in many tackle shops.

Other tinned baits available from the supermarket that can catch carp include beans, peas and chickpeas.

Smaller particles such as hempseed and bird seed mixes, although too small for the hook, can be introduced to the swim as a bed of feed to attract the carp with a larger bait fished over the top.

A mixture of different particles can be used to provide variety, with a few pellets or broken boilies added so the carp get used to eating samples of your hook bait.

Some particles can be purchased from animal feed distributors, but these have to be prepared by soaking or boiling before use.

Many fisheries have banned some particle baits, especially nuts, because if incorrectly prepared they are dangerous to carp. Always check the rules to make sure a bait is allowed before you use it.

DYES AND FLAVOURINGS

A range of dyes and flavourings is available to enhance your baits and you will find a selection of these at your local tackle shop.

Many carp anglers dip their baits in flavouring to increase the leakage of flavour into the swim. This practice is known as 'glugging'.

MEAT

Tinned luncheon meat cut into cubes or prepared with a bait punch is a popular carp bait on many waters. It can be put directly on the hook or fished on a hair rig.

Sections of hard spicy sausage fished on a hair rig can also be successful.

BREAD

Bread is a very versatile bait. It can be cut into cubes, flakes torn from the middle of a loaf can be pressed on to the shank of a hook and crust can be used as a floating bait.

It can also be kneaded with a little water into a paste and enhanced with dyes and flavourings.

NATURAL BAITS

A bunch of maggots can be an effective carp bait when loose fed maggots are introduced to the swim. As maggots will crawl away and bury themselves in leaves and silt it is best to introduce them little and often during the session.

Worms of all kinds are a very effective carp bait on some waters. Large lobworms and dendrobaenas can be fished whole, or cut in half and smaller worms such as redworms can be fished two or three on a hook.

Sea food baits such as shrimps, prawns and cockles will also catch carp.

FLOATING BAITS

For surface fishing there is a range of floating baits to try.

Commercially prepared floaters are available in a range of flavours and colours and can be bought from many tackle shops.

Dog and cat biscuits have accounted for many carp catches. They can be soaked in water to make them soft enough to hook or drilled for use on a hair rig.

ARTIFICAL BAITS

Many manufacturers now produce a range of artificial baits for carp fishing. These are usually made of plastic and both floating and sinking versions are available.

There is an artificial version for just about every kind if bait including maggots, worms, sweetcorn, dog biscuits, pellets, boilies and bread.

Although they have no nutritional value and cannot be digested, they can be very successful when fished over a bed of feed. Some anglers flavour artificial baits to increase their attractiveness.

Floating artificial baits can be fished on a hair alongside real baits to make them buoyant, for example you could fish a floating grain of artificial sweetcorn between two real grains of sweetcorn on a hair rig.

CASTING TECHNIQUES

There are two main casting techniques that you will need to master, the overhead cast, and the underarm cast.

The overhead cast is the one you will use for mid and long range casting while the underhand cast is used when you just need to swing a bait into the margins.

OVERHEAD CAST

To begin the cast, let out enough line so that you can comfortably swing the tackle by moving the rod backwards and forwards. Open the bail arm of the spool so that the line can run off, and prevent this by trapping the line against the spool with your finger.

Next, lift the rod to a vertical position so that it is pointing straight up. The next part requires practice to get the timing just right so don't worry if your initial attempts don't go too well.

Imagine that you are standing next to a large clock face, and the rod is currently pointing to 12 o'clock.

In one fluid movement, swing the tackle behind you by moving the rod sharply back so that it is pointing at between 10 and 11 o'clock, and then immediately move the rod sharply forwards so that it is pointing at between 1 and 2 o'clock. Stop the rod, and release the line by lifting your finger off the spool.

If you get the timing right, the tackle should be propelled away from you towards the place where you want to fish and if the spool is loaded correctly, line should come off the spool freely.

When the tackle is a few inches above the water, drop the rod tip to between 3 and 4 o'clock, and the tackle should land gently on the surface without causing too much disturbance.

The most difficult part of the cast is timing the release of the line correctly. If you release too early, the line will fly up in the air without the necessary power, and will land in a heap. Release too late, and the tackle will not achieve the required distance and will be driven with excessive force into the water.

To accurately cast on the same line each time, it helps to aim towards a distant object such as a tree on the far bank.

UNDERHAND CAST

To begin the cast, assuming you are right handed, hold the rod in your right hand, open the bail arm of the reel, and let out enough line from the rod tip so that with your left hand you can comfortably hold the line just above the hook.

Hold the rod across your body while keeping the line under tension with your left hand, and then flick the rod towards the water so that it is pointing directly away from you, at the same time releasing the line held in your left hand.

You should find that the tackle is propelled towards the place you want to fish, and if you get enough power into the cast, and get your timing right, line should flow off the spool.

Timing of this cast can be difficult at first, but with practice you will find that it becomes second nature. As your skills progress you will find that you can achieve this cast holding the rod at different angles to avoid bank side vegetation and other obstacles.

PLAYING, LANDING AND RELEASING CARP

This chapter deals with everything that happens from the point that you get a bite or run to when you return the carp to the water.

STRIKING OR SETTING THE HOOK

It is not usually necessary to do more than apply firm pressure set the hook at the start of a run if you are using a semi-fixed bolt rig as the carp will be swimming away from you strongly .

This is often the case when fishing other rigs too as carp will often set off on a run as soon as they feel the hook.

A firmer pull against the carp may be necessary if it is moving slowly or appears to have stopped, but you should never strike with a strong jerking action as you risk breaking your line or pulling the hook out of the carp.

When margin fishing you will often not get a run and will need to strike as soon as you see the bite. Again, a firm pull to set the hook should be all that is needed.

PLAYING CARP

When you hook a large carp, do not try to bully it out of the water as quickly as possible, your aim is to tire the fish so that when all of the fight has gone out of it, you can draw it safely over the landing net.

Large carp will try to swim away from you as fast as they can when they are hooked, or soon after as they feel resistance. You will usually need to give line to prevent a break or the hook pulling free and this can be done in two ways.

The slipping clutch, if correctly set, allows the spool to rotate to give line when the pull from the carp is approaching that which would break the line.

An alternative is to allow the fish to take line under pressure by winding the reel backwards. Many anglers use a combination of the two, using judgment to determine when giving line by back winding is necessary.

Make sure the slipping clutch is set to just below the breaking strain of the line. Too slack and you will struggle to recover line, too tight and you risk a break.

Playing a carp is a little like a tug of war match. You give a little, you gain a little until eventually the fish starts to tire. To gain the maximum advantage from your tackle it is essential that you use the rod to cushion the lunges of the fish, so most of the time you should hold it high. This applies maximum pressure on the fish, and also prevents it from coming too high in the water before it is ready for the net.

The exception to this is when you need to stop a carp from reaching an obstruction such as a weed bed or some tree roots. If you lock down the reel and try to stop the fish by holding the rod high you may pull out the hook or break the line. When you need to stop a fish in this way, drop the rod tip so you are applying 'side strain'. Usually this will force the fish up nearer the surface and is often enough to make it change direction away from the snag.

Learning to play a carp well is something that only experience can teach you, but with perseverance you will develop an instinct for when a fish is ready to be brought to the net.

LANDING CARP

When a carp is tired you will notice that its lunges and runs become weaker and shorter. This can be the most dangerous part of the fight as the carp will be closer and nearer the surface and you have only a short amount of line between you and the fish.

Very often, a carp that has been brought to the surface will make a desperate lunge for freedom as soon as it sees you or the net, so be prepared to give more line and continue the fight when this happens.

Eventually the carp will be beaten and will turn sideways on the surface. Now is the time to slip the net under it and draw the net back from the water.

Do not drag the carp a long distance to the net, try to get the net close to the carp and draw it over the lip of the net in a steady controlled movement. When fishing rivers you may need to position the net a little downstream of the carp and allow the current to take it over the net. Never try to pull a beaten carp against the current as that is a sure way of pulling out the hook.

Once the carp is in the net, draw the net back in the water to ensure the fish is safely in the folds. You should then disengage the bale arm on the reel and place the rod in its rest so you have both hands free to lift the net.

Do not lift the net out of the water while you are still holding the end of the pole, instead, slide the pole backwards until you can safely lift the net out of the water by gripping it on both sides.

UNHOOKING CARP

Carp should always be supported on a soft well padded mat for unhooking. Carry the carp to the unhooking mat while it is still in the landing net and carefully transfer it to the mat.

Be careful when unhooking carp not to grip them too tightly, and only handle them with damp hands to prevent removal of slime.

Carp will usually be hooked in the lip or just inside the mouth. It is best to use forceps to grip the shank of the hook and gently slide it out of the fish rather than using your fingers. This gives you more control and a better grip on the hook.

It should take only gentle pressure to remove a barbless hook, in fact hooks sometimes fall out in the landing net when tension on the line has been removed.

CARP CARE

Carp should be kept out of water for as little time as possible.

If there is any visible damage to the carp, either from the hook hold or abrasions sustained while you were playing it, apply a small amount of antiseptic to the affected area following the manufacturers instructions.

When handling a carp, for example when transferring it to a sling for weighing, always do so with wet hands and carry the carp as low to the ground as possible to avoid damage if it slips out of your hands.

WEIGHING CARP

Care is required when weighing carp both to protect the fish and to ensure that the scales record an accurate weight.

Scales should be suspended by the handle or ring at the top and zeroed with a wetted weigh sling attached to the hook.

The sling should then be removed and taken to the unhooking mat from which the carp is transferred into the sling.

Secure the sling and place the sling on the hook. Make sure the scales are suspended securely and hanging vertically, then note the weight.

If you are now ready to return the carp, carry it to the water while still in the weight sling. If you intend to take a photograph, first return the carp to the unhooking mat.

PHOTOGRAPHING CARP

If you are planning to photograph the carp you catch, set up your camera gear when you tackle up so the carp is not kept out of water while you retrieve your camera equipment from your bag.

If you want a photograph of you holding the carp, it is best to ask someone else to take the photograph for you unless you have specialist camera equipment that allows you to set up the camera on a tripod or pole and a switch that allows you to activate the camera remotely.

If there is no one nearby who can take the photograph and you do not have the necessary camera equipment, photograph the carp while it is lying safely on the unhooking mat.

The photograph should be taken with you kneeling behind the unhooking mat while supporting the carp no more than a few inches above the mat.

The person taking the photograph should also be kneeling to get the right perspective. Make sure they are lined up and ready to take the photograph before you lift the carp.

To lift the carp, support it by holding it at the head just in front of the pectoral fins and the tail, just in front of the tail fin. The carp may struggle when you lift it, so be prepared for this so you can support it or return it gently to the mat if necessary.

Do not hold the carp against your body as it could be damaged by zips or buttons and do not grip it too tightly.

After the photograph has been taken, gently lower the carp back on to the unhooking mat in preparation for returning it to the water.

RETURNING CARP TO THE WATER

After unhooking and weighing, the carp should be carried to the water in a weigh sling or landing net unless your unhooking mat has handles and is designed to cradle carp when returning them to the water.

Carry the carp to the water, getting as low as you can and carefully slide the carp from the sling or net into the water while supporting it gently by loosely holding the wrist of its tail.

Continue to hold the carp until it has recovered at which point it will give a strong flick of its tail and swim off strongly.

Before you continue fishing, take a few minutes to tidy up and make sure that your unhooking, weighing and photographing equipment is ready for the next carp.

CARP FISHING ON LAKES, PITS AND POOLS

On many fisheries, the most popular swim is the one nearest the car park. If it isn't that one, it's probably the first one that has a comfortable level bank and no obstructions to get in the way of casting.

It's surprising how many anglers choose a swim based on their own convenience and comfort and give little or thought to whether it is a suitable habitat to attract carp.

Location isn't the only thing that will decide whether you catch carp, you need to fish the swim correctly using the right tackle and good bait, but if you pick a swim that the carp don't visit, you won't catch any.

Having given no thought to the likelihood of their swim containing carp, or if it does where they are likely to be found and to feed, many anglers move their tackle into the swim with the subtlety and finesse of a labourer moving rubble on a building site.

Once everything is set up they bait their rods, cast them as far as they can into the water and follow that with a ton of bait. They then settle down behind their alarms and wait.

If carp fishing was that simple, everyone would be able to catch carp and there wouldn't be any need for this book!

So the first thing you need to do when you arrive at a fishery is decide where to fish.

If you're lucky enough to arrive at a water to find that there are few or no anglers present, you can take your time looking all around the fishery.

If you arrive to find that some parts of the fishery are crowded with many anglers already there, concentrate your search for a swim in less crowded areas. Carp will often move into these areas if they have been disturbed by the activity of other anglers.

When looking around the fishery, move carefully and quietly, keeping back from the edge of the water. Carp can't hear you, but they can feel vibrations from heavy footsteps and if you are too close to the water they will see you before you see them.

Ideally you will see signs of carp to help you to choose a swim. You may see carp near the surface, or see signs of feeding in the form of bubbles rising to the surface.

In clear water you may be able to see carp in the margins and another good sign is movement of water lilies or reeds caused by carp brushing against them.

If you can't see any signs of carp, you will have to choose a swim by 'reading the water'. Another term for this is 'watercraft' which, simply put, is the ability that experienced anglers have of being able to recognise swims where there is a good prospect of catching carp by observation.

You can get a head start on a water and save a lot of time by asking for advice about a fishery in your local tackle shop and talking to other anglers you meet on the bank, but there is no substitute for being able to read a water for yourself.

Over time, you will develop watercraft as a skill that you apply instinctively, but for now I can tell you some of the features that make good fish holding areas.

Carp like cover where they can feel safe and that they can swim into if they feel threatened. They also like a ready supply of food.

Patches of lily pads, weeds and rushes provide both and are likely carp holding areas.

Overhanging trees provide a sense of security and the roots below the surface of the water provide a place of safety.

Islands, especially with overhanging trees are good carp holding areas. Carp like to patrol the margins where there is often a good supply of food and the shelves of islands are essentially the same as the margins on your own bank, but without disturbance from anglers.

After selecting your swim it's time to set up and start fishing.

Position your chair, rod rests or rod pods, bait table, landing net, unhooking mat and shelter if you're using one, as quietly as possible. It's best to do this before setting up your rods so you can immediately place them on rests where you don't risk standing on them.

Hopefully you've identified some areas likely to produce carp when choosing the swim and are ready to set up the rigs and start fishing.

Experienced carp anglers have a rod set up for finding features on the bed of the water using a marker float. This is a valuable technique to learn, but on well stocked club waters and commercial carp fisheries, especially with everything else to learn, its not usually necessary.

A good approach in a swim with no obvious features is to fish one rod fairly close to your own bank and another further out in the water.

If you are fishing a rod close to your own bank, perhaps near to a feature such as a weed bed or lily pads, a float rig set up using the lift method can be effective.

For fishing further out, the running leger rig or semi-fixed bolt rig are good rigs to start with, or the helicopter rig if you need a long cast.

Cast your rigs to the areas of the swim you have chosen. Allow the rigs to settle and close the bail arm of the reel.

For float rigs, sink the line by putting the rod top below the surface and flicking the rod sharply upwards, If you find this difficult and can cast beyond where you want to fish, you can sink the line with a quick turn or two of the reel handle instead.

If you are using the lift method, bites will usually result in the float rising out of the water, but it may sometimes go under, or move to the side.

Place the rod in rests with the rod tip near the surface and take up any slack line.

For a leger rig, place the rod in the rest and take up any slack line. Attach the bobbin to the line and if you are using an alarm make sure that the line is passing over the roller . Finally, put the reel into free spool mode.

When you get a bite the bobbin will either lift or fall depending on whether the carp is swimming away from or towards you. If you are using an alarm it will be activated and if the fish sets off on a run the alarm will continue to sound.

If you are using a running line rig and the bobbin moves up or down a little then stops, or you hear occasional bleeps from the alarm, it may be that the carp are dropping the bait. A switch to the semi-fixed bolt rig may produce more positive results.

Striking bites, playing and landing fish and returning them to the water is covered in a later chapter.

Next its time to put in some bait. A good approach on club lakes and commercial carp fisheries is to feed a small amount of bait regularly.

If you are fishing a float rig, you can simply throw or catapult a pouch full of bait so it lands around the float.

It is not so easy to judge where your bait is when legering at any distance, so you can either catapult a few free offerings around the area you are fishing, or use a PVA stringer or PVA bag to put bait in the swim when you cast.

How often you feed from this point on with be determined by how often you get bites. If you get a bite, whether you hook the fish or not, you should feed when you re-cast.

If you are not getting bites, or waiting a long time between fish, it pays to top the swim up from time. If you are fishing pellets or particles, introduce another 6 to 10 on each line every 10 to 15 minutes, but be more sparing if you are fishing with boilies.

It can pay on club lakes and commercial fisheries to fish small or medium sized boilies over loose fed pellets or particles with a few broken boilies.

This regular feeding approach works on club and commercial fisheries because there is a high density of fish in the water and fish are likely to be moving through your swim eating your bait regularly.

When you progress to less densely stocked fisheries in pursuit of larger carp, a different feeding approach will usually be required as there may be long periods when there are no feeding carp in your swim.

Your approach then will usually be to prepare a bed of bait around your hook bait for the carp to settle and feed on when they pass through your swim.

CARP FISHING ON CANALS AND DRAINS

Canals and drains are essentially long narrow stillwaters. They do flow a little and areas near lock gates on canals with a lot of boat traffic can be moving much of the time, but as a general rule they can be fished like a stillwater.

While most if not all canals and drains contain some carp, they are not numerous and long stretches may hold no carp at all.

Although carp do sometimes travel long distances, they will often remain in the same area for long periods if conditions and availability of food suit them, so if you can locate carp on a scouting trip there is a good chance they will be in the same stretch a few days later.

You can locate carp on canals and drains by looking for the same signs as on stillwaters; large fish moving on or near the surface, bubbles indicating feeding and disturbance of reeds or water lilies.

Canals usually have a bed of silt and debris into which a running leger or semi-fixed bolt rig would sink, so a chod rig with a buoyant bait may be required.

Apart from the possibility that you may need a buoyant hook bait, any bait should be suitable, but if there are a lot of other small fish present such as roach, they are likely to take small baits so you may need to use larger baits such as boiles or cubes of luncheon meat.

You will have to judge how much to feed and whether to adopt a stalking approach based on your observations of the carp on scouting visits.

If you can determine the patrolling habits of the carp, putting down a bed of feed for them to find when they pass by could be effective. Alternatively, if they seem to remain in quite a small area, a little and often feeding approach may be called for.

CARP FISHING ON RIVERS

Many rivers now hold carp, many having escaped into river systems following the heavy floods of recent years.

As with canals and drains though, they are not numerous so locating them is the key to successful river carp fishing. You are most likely to find carp in slow moving rivers and the slower parts of rivers with a medium flow.

Look for the usual signs of carp activity; carp cruising near the surface, bubbles indicating feeding and disturbance of reeds or water lilies

If you are unable to locate carp, but you know they are present in a stretch of river, you can try fishing for them in areas likely to hold them such as slow tree lined bends, weir pools, weed and reed beds and near to moored boats.

You do not need a complicated rig for river carp fishing, a simple running leger rig will usually be suitable.

Rivers contain a lot of other species of fish, so small baits such as pellets and particles are not suitable for the hook and you will need to use a larger bait such as a boilie, worm or luncheon meat.

Particles can be used as an attractor though, and even though they will attract other fish into the swim, that is not necessarily a bad thing as they could in turn attract carp.

It is difficult to be selective about what takes your bait when you are river fishing as large fish of most species will readily take any bait that a carp will, so you will likely catch other species too.

STALKING TACTICS

Stalking can be one of the most exciting forms of carp fishing. Very often you can see the fish you are targeting and even watch them as they take the bait, while you are doing your best to keep completely still and out of sight.

Stalking isn't possible on all waters as on popular waters most or all swims will occupied, but if you can stalk a few swims without upsetting other anglers on the water, its a great way to catch bonus carp.

If you're already set up in a swim and decide to have an hour or so stalking, you must reel in your rods first. Even though you may be fishing with bite alarms and are only a swim away, you'll still be considered to have left your rods unattended which isn't allowed.

When stalking you need to be stealthy. You're looking for carp in the margins and heavy footsteps or the sight of you looming over the water will send them running for cover.

Approach each likely swim with caution. If there are fish in the swim, its usually not a good idea to disturb them by dropping bait on top of them.

Instead, wait a few minutes to see if they move away. If they do, you can drop in a few free samples of your hook bait and move on, or you can drop in your rig and wait for them to return.

Even if you don't see any fish, its a good idea to drop a few baits into likely areas to try on your way back.

If the water isn't clear enough to see into, drop baits into likely carp holding and feeding areas such as near lily pads, weed beds and under overhanging trees.

A simple free-lined rig is usually best for stalking as you can drop a the rig into the water with little disturbance. If you need more casting weight or want to pin the line to the bottom you can add shot or blobs of tungsten putty to the hook link.

Either watch the bait for bites or if you can't see the bait because you're having to keep out of sight, watch the line and strike if it straightens out.

The lift method with a small waggler float can also be a successful stalking rig and can be very effective when the water is coloured.

The best times to stalk for carp are early mornings and late evenings. Carp become more confident as the light starts to fall and will often move into the margins in search of food.

NIGHT AND LONG SESSION CARP FISHING

The same tackle, techniques and rigs that you use for fishing during the day can be used for night fishing, but as soon as the sun goes down and night descends, fishing and moving around your swim becomes much more difficult.

In the section on carp fishing tackle I covered night fishing essentials, but here is a reminder:

- Take a shelter suitable for the time of year. A lightweight shelter is fine for the summer, but you'll need a bivvy for the winter.

- Make sure you have a torch and preferably a head torch too, with spare batteries for each.

- You wont be comfortable sleeping in a chair, so a take a bedchair and a sleeping bag suitable for the time of year; lightweight for the summer and more thickly padded for the winter.

- Make sure you have warm clothing you can put on to keep you warm when the temperature drops.

- Take cooking equipment so you can have hot drinks and meals and enough food and water for the session.

- Store food, milk and spare bait in a cool bag to keep it fresh.

It is essential that you are organised and have everything you need to hand, preferably on a bivvy table next to you.

Rigs are difficulty to tie up in the dark, so have several rigs made up and near to hand in case you have to replace a rig during the night.

In the chapter on playing, landing and releasing carp I covered the importance of setting up your unhooking station before you start fishing. It is even more important at night that you don't have to hunt around for your unhooking mat and forceps in the dark.

Before it gets dark, pick a marker on the far bank such as a tree and use it as a casting and baiting target. You will be able to make out the silhouette of large far bank features on all but the darkest nights, so you will have something to aim at when casting and feeding in the dark.

You won't be able to see your bobbins at night, so attaching chemical lights or isotopes is a good idea. You can attach them to other items so you can find them too, such as your landing net.

Keep your bait out of reach of scavengers. You may not see them during the day, but rats and other rodents will be active at night and would soon eat their way though anything they can reach.

Early mornings just as it is starting to get light is a great time for stalking in the margins.

Carp feel more confident and move in closer to the bank in search of food when its dark and they will often still be there when its just starting to get light so its a great time to catch a bonus carp.

Have a stalking rod already set up and some bait and tackle essentials ready to go in a bait bucket so you just have to pick up your landing net and go looking for some carp.

CARP FISHING IN WINTER

Carp are much less active in winter and weather conditions, especially at night can be very uncomfortable, but if you're dedicated enough you can still catch carp.

In the chapter on night fishing I covered the importance of shelter, keeping warm and being able to make hot food and drinks, so I wont repeat that here, but do make sure that you have good thermal clothing and boots to keep you warm.

Tackle and techniques that you use in the summer months can be used in the winter, but the fish will be less inclined to feed and more cautious, so you may need to scale down to a smaller hook and possibly a lighter hook link.

Baits should be smaller too and you should only introduce a small amount of bait to the water.

To give yourself the best chance of a carp, fish a water where the fish are known to feed all through the year. Well stocked day ticket waters and commercial fisheries are more likely to produce than lightly stocked waters that can be hard to catch on in the summer.

Carp are less likely to move around in the winter, so if you see signs of fish somewhere else on the water you'll have more chance of catching if you move than if you wait for them to come to you.

Winter fishing can be uncomfortable and not everyone has the will to do it, but if you can summon up the enthusiasm you will be on the bank when few others are, sometimes you can even get a whole lake to yourself.

Fish can be few and far between and you'll have blank days, but when you do bank a winter carp it suddenly all seems worth it!

LICENCES AND PERMISSION TO FISH

Anyone aged 12 or over must have a fishing licence to fish for coarse fish. The penalty for being caught fishing without a licence is a fine of up to £2,500.

Full details of current prices can be obtained from the Environment Agency website, where you can also apply for a licence. Licences can also be obtained at post offices.

A licence only allows you to fish legally, it does not mean you can fish anywhere you choose. There are some locations where you can fish for free, but most fishing waters are either owned by fishing clubs that you have to join, or available to fish by purchasing a day ticket.

WHEN YOU CAN FISH

On rivers there is an annual close season for coarse fishing from 15 March to 15 June each year and you are not allowed to fish using coarse fishing methods during that period.

There is no close season for coarse fishing on lakes, canals and ponds so you are legally allowed to fish all year round, but some clubs enforce their own close season, so check the rules for your chosen fishery before setting out.

If you intend to fish at night, which can be a very productive time for many species, check with your local club or fishery to find out if this is allowed, and whether you need to obtain a special night fishing permit.

ABOUT THE AUTHOR

I was born in Oxford in 1959, but spent most of my childhood further north in the West Midlands. I am currently based in Devon in the south west of England, but still have a particular fondness for the Warwickshire and Worcestershire countryside.

I became interested in nature at a young age and spent a lot of my free time and holidays out in the fresh air walking and fishing with friends. I've lived, worked, walked and fished over many parts of Britain and that early interest has developed into a fascination for the natural world.

As well as writing, I collect and restore vintage fishing tackle. I like to fish with cane rods, centrepin reels and quill floats and when I'm not writing I like nothing more than to spend a few hours on a country stream fishing and watching birds, butterflies, and other wild creatures in their natural environment.

You can contact me and find out about my other books and current projects at my website: www.paulduffield.me.uk.

Printed in Great Britain
by Amazon

79334924R00045